Stray Writings

Stray Writings

Raj Kumar Bhatia

PRABHAT
PAPERBACKS

Published by
PRABHAT PAPERBACKS
An imprint of Prabhat Prakashan Pvt. Ltd.
4/19 Asaf Ali Road,
New Delhi-110002 (INDIA)
e-mail: prabhatbooks@gmail.com

ISBN 978-93-5521-309-9
STRAY WRITINGS
by Shri Raj Kumar Bhatia

Edition
First, 2022

Price
₹ 200.00 (Rupees Two Hundred only)

Printed at
R-Tech Offset Printers, Delhi

Dedicated to

Prof. Yashwant Rao Kelkar

the real architect of
Akhil Bharatiya Vidyarthi Parishad (ABVP)
and my third Guru in
public life

Preface

Quite in young age I started expressing my views through letters to the editors in Hindi newspapers. Writing became a regular feature for me when I had to write in Hindi and English on ABVP (Akhil Bharatiya Vidyarthi Parishad) related matters after I joined the organisation. Then came the phase of expressing myself on different subjects both in Hindi and English in newspapers and periodicals, more in Hindi than English, and in English I wrote the most in year 2004 courtesy Organiser weekly. Then off and on I kept expressing in both the languages.

In English writing it was a kind of break for me when I wrote for Indian Express in 1993 on issue of demolition of Babri structure in Ayodhya and in Hindustan Times in 1997 on outcome of Delhi University Students' Union (DUSU) election. As I was deeply involved in ABVP I analysed DUSU election results twice later in Pioneer daily and Organiser weekly also.

Writing a 3 part article in Organiser weekly in June 2004 soon after Lok Sabha election was my peak and I felt like having become a litterateur in same year when two of my brief writings in Organiser on Gujarat and related to a social organisation were published.

Last piece I wrote on my own was in 2011 in Organiser and then it was only in 2020 when I wrote for Indian Express on demand and explicit assurance that my labour would not go waste.

I wrote very few letters to the editor in English as my success rate was not encouraging. This book contains three letters which were not published but which I consider as worth presenting to the readers.

Few months ago I aspired that my writings be presented in a book. I am obliged to Prabhat Prakashan for fulfilling my wish.

—Raj Kumar Bhatia

Contents

The Man and His Mission

Shri Guruji: The Second Most Powerful Personality of the 20th Century India

Organising the Hindu society and establishing Bharat as a Hindu *rashtra* was Shri Guruji's mission. The mission was bequeathed to him by his leader and founder of RSS Dr. Hedgewar whom he succeeded as the head of the organisation in 1940. The succession was not merely a case of one head taking the place of the other. It was, on the one hand, an example of same mission being taken over by a follower from his leader, and on the other of mutual acknowledgement of each other's superiority by two great personalities. Perhaps such examples are rarely found where the follower surpasses his leader in the pursuit of their common goal.

Dr. Hedgewar created RSS essentially to achieve the goal of country's independence. Shri Guruji

---

The article wrote for Panchnad Research Institute journal in 2006 during Shri Guruji's centenary celebrations.

enlarged the goal by adding to it the rebuilding of post-independence India. Dr. Hedgewar tried to organise Hindu society because he thought it was necessary for achieving independence. Shri Guruji organised the society hammering the point that Hindutva was the lifeline of India's nationhood. Shri Guruji did not stop there. He underlined the significance of Hindutva even for the whole world. That is why he took the personal initiative in establishing Vishwa Hindu Parishad [VHP] which was meant to organise the Hindus all over the world.

Perhaps to Shri Guruji the trait of outshining the leader (Dr. Hedgewar) had come because of three reasons. Firstly, because of the impact of a similar and much glaring recent example of Swami Ramakrishna Paramhansa and his disciple Swami Vivekananda. The latter had surpassed his guru in spreading the message of spirituality. As a spiritual person Shri Guruji also belonged to the Ramakrishna order and was deeply influenced by Swami Vivekananda who was just like his guru being the *gurubhai* of his formal guru Swami Akhandananda. Secondly, since Shri Guruji was essentially a spiritual person who had faith in the rich Hindu tradition of complete surrender by the disciple or follower before the guru or leader. Thirdly, Shri Guruji himself was an informal guru for many persons. His nickname of 'Guruji' was not a coincidence. It was the outcome of his spiritual personality. So the guru in him very well knew what his obligations were as a disciple.

Once the mission was identified there was no looking back for Shri Guruji. It was a focussed single-minded journey of nearly four decades treaded towards the goal day in and day out. Several things were done by the missionary towards the fulfilment of the goal. The RSS was built as a mighty organisation, the do's and don'ts of the organisation were clearly laid down, swayamsevaks were regularly enlightened about the goal, necessary complimentary institutions were created with competent persons assigned the tasks and supporters of the goal were cultivated all over the country. Thus rose the largest NGO of the country and perhaps of the world on the national scene and it later on came to be popularly known as the 'Sangh Parivar'.

Shri Guruji left for his heavenly abode 33 years ago and he also led RSS for the same number of years. He traversed the length and breadth of the country so deeply and so many times that he is credited for having been the first person to do so. This way he acquired first-hand knowledge of the needs of the country on the basis of which he made several important contributions in the life of the nation. If Mahatma Gandhi influenced the socio-political life of India most during the first half of the 20th century Shri Guruji would be remembered for having done so in the other half. Some of his contributions like making the King of Jammu & Kashmir agree to accession with India, advising non-Sikhs of Punjab to declare Punjabi as their mother tongue at the time of 1961 Census and forewarning the country about China's aggression on India are widely known. That he assigned Shri Eknath Ranade, one of the top and best Sangh leaders, to the task of the construction of the Vivekanand Rock Memorial is also known. His less known but equally important contributions were assigning the tasks of establishing a nationalist labour organisation and creating a network of contacts with Hindus spread all over the world to two of the best swayamsevaks of the Sangh – Shri Dattopant Thengadi and Shri Chaman Lal. Yet the following contributions of Shri Guruji may be rated as the best ones in view of their long-lasting and deeper impact:

He passionately advocated supreme patriotism amongst the Sangh Swayamsevaks in particular and public in general. For him patriotism was a one-way affair. No self-interest and 'do and die' for the country. Nations become great only when such a spirit exists amongst its people, he believed. He often used to call for unadulterated patriotism.

Shri Guruji was quite clear about the limitations of power politics in respect of the development of the country. He firmly believed that a society's progress depends basically on the commitment towards it of its average members. The governmental power at best can accelerate the process. So he scrupulously kept RSS away from power politics. Though he sent the finest of Sangh pracharaks like Shri Deendayal Upadhyaya to become the key organiser of Jana Sangh yet he always called for the distance that RSS was to maintain from the Jana Sangh despite the ideological closeness between the two organisations.

For Shri Guruji publicity was the last thing to be worried about by RSS; rather, RSS was to shun publicity because it was more of a detriment in the pursuit of the goal. The goal was to arouse duty consciousness amongst the people which could become possible when there existed no ambition of name and fame in the life of a person and even amongst the organisation.

And he applied the above prescription first to himself. He had strong aversion to personal glorification and publicity. Scores of examples can be found in his life to this effect. But the most shining of them was his last letter written just before his death in which he wrote that 'glorification of a person has no place in Sangh work and increasing the importance of a person and raising his memorials, except for the founder of Sangh (i.e. Dr. Hedgewar), is not necessary'. Had he not written that explicit note, this country perhaps would have witnessed raising of hundreds of his statues all over the country by now. Let us not forget that apart from being the Sarsanghchalak of RSS, Shri Guruji was a highly respected person because of his dedication, intellect and oratory. Also, during his pretty long tenure as Sarsanghchalak of RSS the organisation reached every nook and corner of the country and became a very powerful social organisation. This fact alone was enough for Shri Guruji to earn name and fame if he had so desired. He could have earned name and fame even at the international level because of the work of Vishwa Hindu Parishad. The creation of VHP was Shri Guruji's brainchild. Other than RSS the only organisation, in the building of which Shri Guruji took personal interest and put in his extraordinary efforts, was the VHP. Shri Guruji was the virtual founder of the organisation and this he did almost single handedly. He succeeded in bringing a variety of top leaders of Hindu sects together and launched VHP to create a forum for Hindus at the international level. This effort of Shri Guruji raised him in the esteem of many Hindus living all over the world.

There was one more reason which could have brought him name and fame and that was possible because of developments in the political field. In the last few years of his life he became a renowned personality due to the political clout achieved by Sangh swayamsevaks in politics. Jana Sangh became an important national party after its successes in 1967.

All the above-mentioned developments made Shri Guruji as one of the most powerful leaders of the country. Yet the developments only increased his humility, rather than going to his head.

The Man and His Mission

One more personal example of Shri Guruji was noteworthy. He chose the unusual path of becoming a non-saffron clad *sanyasi*. He was a spiritualist of first order for he had acquired the full eligibility for being initiated into *sanyas* by Ramakrishna Math. Some people are of the opinion that had Shri Guruji become a *sanyasi* he would have been ranked equal to Swami Vivekananda and Sri Aurobindo. Yet he decided to adopt the different path, perhaps at the asking of his leader (Dr. Hedgewar). He preferred to fulfil the worldly needs of the country in place of his personal spiritual urge. His was a rare case of a *sanyasi* and a non-*sanyasi* rolled into one.

□

Shri Guruji Centenary Thoughts: Contemporary Relevance of Shri Guruji's Ideology

Shri Guruji's ideology was not different from that of his leader Dr. Hedgewar. The latter had founded RSS and had chosen the former to succeed him. Though not formal but virtually he was a disciple of Dr. Hedgewar (He had taken to *sanyas* as a formal disciple of Swami Vivekananda's *gurubhai* Swami Akhandananda) whose path he never deviated from.

His ideology comprised of two elements: (i) *Bharat* i.e. India is a Hindu *rashtra* and (ii) to make it strong, the Hindu society should be organised.

The relevance of his ideology can be judged with respect to two time periods – the pre and the post Independence ones. The relevance seems to have increased in the latter period than it was in the former. There were four reasons for the relevance in

Published in Organiser weekly on 18 February, 2007.

the first period; they rose to six in the second.

In the pre-Independence period, the ideology was relevant for the following reasons:

1. For some centuries in the past the spirit of nationalism had become very weak in India. It needed to be awakened.
2. As a consequence of first reason the British were ruling the country. They had to be ousted.
3. There existed a virus of minorityism amongst Muslims in national life and it was creating one or the other hurdles in the development of a healthy national life.
4. The ideology of consumerism, in view of the material prosperity of the Western countries, was regarded as the right model to follow by a section of the elite (aptly called Macaulay-*putras*) of the country.

The British left the country in 1947. One of the four reasons was gone. But it gave birth to two new reasons thus raising the number to five. The British did not simply leave the country; they partitioned the nation on the false premise of two-nation theory. The virus of minorityism got two new fangs and the disease became three-dimensional. The original problem continued and its new dimensions cropped up in the form of a) first one, and later two hostile neighbours with Islam being their lifeline; and b) most of the political parties vying for en masse votes of muslims in the elections at various levels, thus legitimising minorityism and derailing the democratic polity of the country.

But one more reason, the sixth one to make Shri Guruji's ideology relevant, was acquiring the shape when we became independent. Marxism became a much attractive ideology for many in the country. In the post-Independence period it harmed the country in more than one way. If on the one hand it stood directly opposed to India's nationhood, on the other it succeeded in creating a powerful and strong elite (Marx-*putras*) in the country, spreading all sorts of ideological confusions. This very elite also succeeded in manoeuvring and manipulating the state apparatus to get entrenched in the body politic of the country, especially in the fields of education and mass communication.

Reverting to Shri Guruji's ideology, how is the concept of Hindu *rashtra* lo be justified? Is Hindu not a religious entity? Should we equate nationalists with a religious community? Why organising of such a community is necessary for the betterment of the country?

Let us first define a Hindu. Perhaps there is no controversy about the origin of the word 'Hindu'. It took birth to signify the nationality of the people living to the south of Sindhu river. The word acquired a religious meaning later on. Today Hindu is given one more meaning also, especially when it is defined through its derivatives of Hinduism or Hindutva. Both these words highlight a certain way of life. So Hindu can be defined in three ways. But are the definitions contradictory? If not, where is the problem?

In all the meanings, one thing is common and that is the land called Hindusthan or Hindustan or Bharat or India. When the original meaning of Hindu is taken, it signifies the nationality of this land. When the religious (it needs elaboration) meaning is taken, it virtually incorporates religions originating from this land.

Lastly, when the 'way of life' meaning is taken, it is the way of life of the people that have lived on this land for long.

Before we proceed further, let the religious meaning be clear. Bharat, i.e. India is home of many religions. The oldest of them is called Hindu. Though other religions have different names, the prominent ones being Buddhism, Jainism and Sikhism, they have many common elements of Hinduism and can safely be termed as one religion. All these religions are quite different from semitic religions, like Christianity and Islam. Tolerance, non-aggressiveness, non-proselytisation, etc. are their common features. The religions can be called Hindu because of the land of their origin, i.e. Hindusthan.

The logic may not be palatable to those who have grown up in intellectually-perverted thinking, especially because of the influence of Left intellectuals. They do not like to go into the origin of the word Hindu. They like to go by its religious meaning. But a more significant thing is that religion for them is a dangerous phenomenon and is an irrational and an unscientific trait of human beings. Even if they don't condemn religion or religiosity, they consider different religions as being antagonistic. When antagonism is not important for them, then putting Hinduism at par with Christianity and Islam becomes a compulsive faith for them. They have no patience to delve into the history of growth of religions and to appreciate the differences between them. Nothing surprising. History has the habit of providing power and eminence to irrational and shortsighted persons at one or the other point of time. But it doesn't happen for ever.

A Hindu can be comprehensively defined as a national of Bharat, born and brought up in one or the other religions born in India and who is more or less guided by the way of life evolved in India.

The critics of Shri Guruji's ideology easily accept the third definition of Hindu but it becomes hard for them to swallow the first two definitions. Going by the convenient religious definition, they reject the first one, i.e. of nationality and with respect to religious definition, they apply it to only those people who are popularly known as Hindus. But where are they mistaken?

Their mistake lies either in ignorance or in misconception about the ingredients of Indian nationality and its connection with Hindu religion. They commit this mistake under the ideological influence of Macaulay-*putras* and Marx-*putras*, both of whom succeeded in dominating the intellectual climate of the 20th-century Bharat. The ideologies of capitalism and Marxism had their free play in our country in the last century. Both of them are materialistic philosophies which have sought to rule, not only India, but the whole world. Of the two, Marxism is a more deadly ideology. It denigrates nationalism and religion both and considers them as inferior human urges. It fails to appreciate that nationalism does not necessarily negate internationalism. Religion for it is an opium of masses. It overlooks the fact that most of the people, including the educated, enlightened, modem and scientific persons are religious in their lives and find solace in following one or the other religion. One may not be religious just because he or she believes in the existence of God, one may be so merely because for him religion symbolises spirituality, morality, or the forces which are beyond his comprehension. Marxists fail to distinguish between religious fanaticism and genuine religiosity. India has been a very ancient nation in this world and spirituality has always been its strong feature, so much so that, as rightly said by Swami Vivekananda, one cannot think of India without spirituality. Spirituality, in its turn, is mostly practiced through a religion and in India the oldest such religion has been the Sanatan Dharma or Hinduism. So Indian nationalism and Hindu religion are interconnected. By the same logic, Indian nationalism and other 'Hindu' religions are interconnected. This way India becomes a Hindu *rashtra* and the Hindu society (people belonging to Hindu religions) takes care of Indian nationalism.

In view of the above analysis, Shri Guruji's ideology can be easily understood. For him even a Muslim or Christian was Hindu when the latter considered India his nation and did not consider his nationality being inferior to his religion. Drawing conclusion from the history of India, Shri Guruji found that unless those who were born in Indian religions and were in line with the Indian way of life and had once acquired the epithet of Hindu for their nationality, were made aware of their history, the nation could not be made strong.

□

Demise of a *Rishi*

In my view the RSS's contribution to the national life of India is not its flawless ideology but its huge and vast organisation of selfless and dedicated workers who stand by its ideology and surpass each other in offering their best to the glory of the motherland. As its name itself suggests the organisation is a federation of nationally conscious swayamsevaks i.e. self-motivated workers. The uniqueness of RSS lies in creating, identifying and bringing together such workers in large numbers. Perhaps the RSS is the largest and the strongest NGO, not only of the country, but also of the world. Dattopant Thengadi was one of the topmost members of this largest NGO.

In RSS, a swayamsevak makes his best offering by being (i) an able organiser, (ii) a good leader and (iii) a sound intellectual. Often a swayamsevak is found to possess one or the other of these qualities. Very few possess more than one quality and very very few

Organiser, 7 November, 2004.

possess all the three. Thengadi belonged to the last category and topped the list. He was an intellectual giant, a master organiser and a unique leader.

For a person in public life it becomes difficult to make comparison between great personalities. Nevertheless, even at the cost of sounding subjective, one still does that, especially between those whom he sees closely. Speaking for myself I found Shri Thengadi to be taller than the tallest amongst the swayamsevaks of RSS in recent years.

I don't know how many others had it but I definitely had the fortune of being very close to him. At least that is what I felt. Though he was much older than me yet he always made me feel like a younger brother who could talk to him on equal terms. I had several occasions of talking/interacting with him. Our interactions used to be free and frank and I always felt that he used to open his heart to me.

Thengadi was an intellectual gem. It was very difficult to gauge the depth of his knowledge and information. His knowledge of thoughts expressed by famous foreign philosophers and intellectuals was amazing. Listening to his speeches and reading the books written by him used to be a sheer delight. I felt enriched whenever I heard or read him and eagerly used to look forward to getting such opportunities.

Thengadi was an organiser par excellence. The more perfect a person is in human reading and in his dealing, the better organiser he will prove. An organiser should not make the mistake of not knowing both the qualities and the weaknesses of a person since, exceptions apart, most people have both of them. An organiser should not be carried away with the latter's qualities nor be ignorant of his weaknesses. Thengadi never faltered on this front.

Thengadi was a first-rate leader in the true spirit of the letter and not a run-of-the-mill one. Though he never craved for name and fame, he still was conscious about his role as a leader. A leader provides vision and direction to the people. He leads by his deeds, not by his words. He removes false notions and confusions from the minds of the people and makes them tread on the right path. Three of his oft-repeated remarks are worth quoting: (i) short cut cuts a person short, (ii) though a path may be long but if that is the only path, then it is the shortest path, and (iii) publicity is no substitute for an organisation.

Thengadi was a real rishi (saint).

□

K.R. Malkani: Journalism of Conviction

Though I had known Malkani before the clamp-down of Emergency in 1975 in the country, I could know his greatness while we were together in Tihar Jail as MISA detenus during that period. Per chance a ward, which could accommodate only a small number of inmates, was to be allotted. A group of young detenus including myself got it. A few elderly persons were also to be added in the group to complete the number. Malkaniji was one of them. To our utter surprise and great pleasure we never felt the age-gap with him. It was an enjoyable company.

Even though Malkaniji was the editor of the *Organiser* weekly, I somehow carried an impression that he was more of a snobbish English journalist than a follower of RSS. I was utterly mistaken. In jail I learnt that he was neither a snob nor an Englishman; on the contrary, he was friendly, sweet and comfortable with people around him and his commitment to RSS ideology and organisational

---

Birth anniversary tribute, Organiser, 28 November, 2004.

discipline was unquestionable. He was as good a swayamsevak as one could be.

The closeness and the kind of personal relationship that both of us developed then continued till he was alive. It was an irony that when I received the news of his death, the Deepavali greeting sent by him to me was on its way.

Malkaniji was a straightforward person who was not calculative in expression of his views and perceptions on matters of social/national importance. Politely but firmly, he would speak out his mind. But when he was made the spokesperson of BJP, it became a necessity for him to be very cautious because he had to speak for the party and not for himself. He performed the duty successfully though not without a few embarrassing incidents.

I had various occasions of meeting and interacting with him, particularly during his tenure at the Deendayal Research Institute (DRI) before he became active in the BJP. I can never forget one very small but interesting episode. I was sitting with him at DRI. Tea was served to us. I had the habit of taking boiling hot tea while he had exactly the opposite habit. I took no time in draining the cup while he took just a few sips. When he noticed this, he said to me, "tea should be sipped, not drunk." He also mentioned that in China handles were not attached to teacups in order to discourage drinking of hot tea because a hot teacup without a handle cannot be held for more than a few seconds.

□

Betrayal of the Sangh (Ayodhya Perspectives)

Scathing attacks have been launched on the RSS, the VHP and the BJP for the demolition of the Ramjanmabhoomi-Babri masjid structure. Though the organisations cannot be fully absolved of the responsibility of the act, much of the criticism is misplaced or prejudiced. Broadly speaking, there are three categories of critics of the RSS school of thought: (i) committed Sangh-baiters, who are pathologically allergic to the RSS and the allied organisations; (ii) genuine critics, who have honest ideological differences with Sangh Parivar; and (iii) shallow intellectuals, who have vague notions about India's history, essentials of its nationhood, definition of secularism, ideals of Sangh Parivar, etc.

No doubt the Parivar failed to keep its promise of not allowing any damage to the disputed structure, but much explanation has been offered by now and

---

Published in *Indian Express* on 7 January, 1993.

they feel betrayed. The fact is that Narasimha Rao betrayed the Sangh leadership. A dispassionate analysis of Rao's performance as Prime Minister, especially in the recent days, convincingly proves that he is confused, indecisive and directionless and has failed in tackling difficult situations. He pushed the Sangh leadership in a corner through his inaction and over action and today he and his party stand cornered more than the Sangh Parivar. While the latter has emerged bruised from the Ayodhya happenings, the former have been totally shattered. Obviously, it was not the responsibility of the karsevaks or the Sangh leaders to save Rao and his party from the predicament in which they find themselves today.

As for their criticism of the Sangh Parivar leaders, critics of the first category have no locus standi, nor should their allegations be taken seriously, though a befitting reply to their criticism is warranted in view of the fact that they have held the intellectual floor of the country for far too long. These critics found nothing positive in the Sangh ideology and the Ayodhya incident of December 6 proved an excellent opportunity for them to indulge in their anti-RSS tirade.

Nations do not live in the present; they live by their past; and great nations have a vision for the future. The problem with this category of people is that they do not want to look into the past. They do not want the story of Islam's entry into India to be unfolded. They place Hinduism and Islam on the same pedestal without enquiry. In their belief that religion is the opium of the masses, most of these critics from the Marxist school of thought equate Hinduism with Islam, irrespective of their past history. This does not mean that they do not believe in history. They do; but their knowledge of history is derived from Marx and the scholars from JNU, who have been liberally fed and pampered by the Congress regimes.

These critics have no inclination to identify the essentials of Indian nationhood since nationalism is a bourgeoise concept for them. They also have no time to go into the history of the RSS and appreciate its contribution because for them the RSS talks of Hinduism, which is just a religion, and religion is a dirty word, and the RSS is nothing but a bandwagon of religious fanatics. To them the Muslim League is acceptable but not the RSS, since the former at least helps them in achieving their foremost goal of power-capturing.

The RSS is least concerned about such critics since it is with them that the RSS has ideological competition. They only help the RSS by propagating their half-baked misconceptions.

It is the second category of critics who need to be taken seriously. Ideological differences apart, the Ayodhya incident has given them the opportunity to catch the Sangh Parivar on the wrong foot. But such critics are over-reacting and are not taking an objective view, though they cannot be blamed for the same. The reason lies in the RSS methodology. Here the chaff needs to be separated from the grain. Perhaps many people don't know that the RSS used to keep itself scrupulously away from publicity. Silent, constructive work and man-to-man contact were the hallmarks of its methodology. Though aspiring to become a mass-movement, it reluctantly opted for techniques that would help it achieve this aim, especially on the image-building front. It often took, to its own disadvantage, no cognisance of false, mischievous and politically-motivated propaganda against itself. As a consequence, it is unnecessarily misunderstood even by well-meaning people. Of late, it is trying to overcome this shortcoming but it will take some time.

Two assurances will not be out of place for such critics. First, the unity and the integrity of the country is the topmost objective of the RSS. The Ayodhya aberration will not deter the RSS from this goal. Second, though the RSS has always stood for Hinduism, it is not anti-Muslim, although it opposes minority politics and wants the wrong of history to be set right.

The third category of critics do not require to be taken seriously. They hardly contribute or matter in the march of the great organisations, like the RSS.

□

Dynasty in Democracy: Malady and Remedy

It is a matter of great satisfaction that yet another general election to the Lok Sabha of the country concluded successfully recently. The individuals or parties may have lost or won, but democracy has definitely emerged as the winner. The proposition may not be easily accepted and may sound hollow when it is weighed in the backdrop of general cynicism towards political parties along with witnessing of ugly faces of the electoral process at the time of elections and limited participation of people in actual voting. Such things prompt many people to raise serious doubts about the legitimacy of elections and desirability of democracy. That is why holding and conclusion of an election becomes an achievement in itself for those who have strong faith in democracy. Without delving much into the subject, it would not

---

Published in Organiser weekly on 6 June, 2004 soon after Lok Sabha election. It was first part of 3 parts article.

be unfair to assert that a dispassionate analysis of the whole affair is bound to lead a thinking citizen to the conclusion that a vast country like ours, with all sorts of diversities, cannot think of living without democracy. So whatever the fate of individuals or parties, the democracy must win.

One can still go further and claim that democracy is proving its worth to the country. A full essay can be written to prove the point but one fresh example should be more than sufficient. The episode of Smt. Sonia Gandhi first staking a claim to the Prime Minister's post and then withdrawing the same will go down in history as a democratic miracle. It was nothing else but effectiveness and vibrancy of a democracy at its zenith. The significance of the episode may take time to be realised but the example is a major milestone in the march of democracy. Though full facts about what compelled Smt. Gandhi to withdraw the claim may or may not come in public knowledge, yet it can be forcefully said that the instant strong voices raised against her efforts to occupy the highest executive post of the country contributed in no small measure in creating an atmosphere of disgust against her attempts and in putting considerable pressure on her. The country was thus saved, courtesy democracy, from experiencing the most embarrassing and humiliating event of seeing a person of foreign origin sitting on the post.

But democracy has yet to achieve several goals.

Two tasks of utmost importance and few others of no less significance are yet to be completed. Democracy will prove its worth in fulfilment of these tasks also, one is sure.

Even though Smt. Gandhi has been stalled from becoming the first person of foreign origin to reach a top executive post of the country, the law to that effect is yet to be enacted. We will witness that being accomplished sooner or later.

The country feels equally disgusted over the perversion of democracy being witnessed in the form of the efforts being made to legitimise dynastic politics in the country. The cry for the induction of Priyanka and Rahul Gandhi in the country's politics and subsequent praises showered on them after their entry into the same highlight the perversion in full measure. Dynastic politics is an anathema to democracy. That a country of over 100 crore and a democracy of over fifty years' standing should be considered beholden to one family for providing rulers to it is a matter of national shame. But one can rest assured that the country would show the door to the family as it has shown to its head.

Of the other important tasks to be accomplished, the foremost one is that of divesting the politics from the malaise of individual-centric parties. The country is experiencing the phenomenon at different levels. A healthy democracy can ill afford this feature. That several political parties have become like sole proprietorship firms of certain political satraps is a matter of serious concern. The malaise will have to be cured.

Freeing the politics from the evil influences of money, muscle, caste and religion, etc. are the other objectives that the democracy of this country has to achieve. A voter casting his vote with full application of his mind and without the influence of narrow considerations is what a healthy democracy requires. India's democracy has been one of its type in the world and is yet to reach a reasonable level of maturity. No democracy in the world is hundred per cent ideal; not even of those countries which are considered strongholds of democracy. As is the considered view of most of the rational thinkers in today's world, democracy is the best amongst all the systems. So strengthening democracy and ridding it from shortcomings becomes the duty of every concerned citizen. Long live democracy!

□

Power Wielding is not Nation Building

With the demise of British raj in 1947, India launched on its march of nation building under its own government. A constitution was adopted on 26 January, 1950 and from 1952, the country started duly voting for its rulers through elections to the Lok Sabha. The fourteenth such election was held recently.

Whenever an election takes place and a certain dispensation takes charge of the government, two distinct moods are seen in the country. Those who have voted for the dispensation feel happy and see a bright future for the country while those who have voted for the other side, feel depressed and see a contrary picture about the country's future. Such a situation can be easily appreciated. After all the electoral verdict and the formation of a government accrue as an outcome of a kind of battle, which

---

Second part of 3 parts article, Organiser, 13 June, 2004.

obviously must end in some winners and some losers. But if the winners become too elated and the losers sulk too much, then what experience is the country likely to go through? Does not an election end up in confusing and dividing the people and projecting a bright as well as gloomy future for the country at the same time? Then what purpose is achieved by holding elections?

It is not that all citizens become so divided. At least three sets of people have different feelings. One set comprises of those who remain indifferent or cynical towards the elections and their outcomes. For them this government or that makes no difference. A substantial proportion of the population belongs to this category. The second set is formed by those who do not get much disturbed since they understand the weaknesses and limitations of the government too well. Their expectations remain close to what the government delivers. The third and last set comprises of those who feel concerned about the government and go through the feelings of joy and sadness, but do not make reconciliatory predictions.

Then what about them who make such predictions leading to sharp divisions amongst themselves, especially when they turn out to be well-meaning, concerned, thinking, enlightened and influential persons of the society? Is it true that we really come across opposite predictions? One has only to experience private and group discussions as well as observe the various debates through media and on public fora. In such a situation what conclusion should one draw from such a scenario? Should the country shelve the elections and bid goodbye to democracy? Does it mean that elections and democracy serve no purpose in the country? Not the least. For paucity of space, it should be sufficient to assert here that elections and democracy are very much needed and they are serving the country well.

An in-depth analysis of the phenomenon of opposite perceptions compels one to conclude that a section of population with such an outlook gets carried away with larger-than-life image of governmental power and places too much faith in the same as far as the progress of the country goes. Not that governmental power carries no importance. It certainly does. The country cannot think of living without a government. Many things, big or small, can be done only by the authority of the government. If nothing else, in the form of the government, the country gets the minimum infrastructure of administration without which the country cannot live even for a day. Crucial tasks of law and order and defence, etc. require round-the-clock existence of the government.

Then why should the governmental power be belittled? Nothing of the sort. Taking cognisance of the governmental limitations does not amount to belittling of the government. India is a vast country with lots of socio-political complexities. One requires a plethora of informations and sound analytical skills to sift the grain from the chaff. Another distinction becomes warranted here. Often well-meaning citizens mix up the two things and live in a make-believe world. They fail in drawing the line between 'what the government can do' and 'what it is likely to do' or between what they wish and what is likely to happen.

No doubt the government can do a lot, but does it mean that those who reach the helm of affairs become automatically committed to that? Our experience of several years indicates to the contrary. Yet quite a few people get deceived by false political posturing. A large number of politicians in India have mastered the art of false image building. Far from reality, they succeed in masquerading as champions of the people's and country's welfare.

But why is it that the government does not do what it can or should? For the answer we have to go back to our history. The government started drifting from its desired path from the time when capture of power came to be considered as the act of nation building itself. Power was to be used for self-interest, but was demanded in the name of the progress of the country. It was needed for serving one's ambition but was asked for, for the fulfillment of social service.

The phenomenon of equating power capturing with nation building began distinctly when Smt. Indira Gandhi captured power in the name of '*garibi hatao*' campaign in 1971. Once begun, the phenomenon never looked back. For contending parties to power, outsmarting each other with making of false promises became a routine affair. So where does the blame exactly lie? Certainly on Smt. Indira Gandhi herself. Though chicken-hearted and misguided citizens shudder to think on this line, it is impossible to escape from the conclusion since the hard facts point to nobody else. One may like it or not, Smt. Indira Gandhi will go down in history as the master destroyer of democratic institutions and unabashed promoter of personality cult, dynastic and vote-bank politics, false posturing and winning of elections with fair or foul means, not disregarding the equal complicity of her party in the guilt.

Till date, the phenomenon knows no stopping. Congress leads in the game and other parties religiously tread on its footprints. The country keeps eagerly awaiting to see the emergence of a genuine, sincere and effective alternative to the Congress politics.

So does it mean that the goal of nation-building will remain captive to the machinations of political powers forever? Not at all. Not for those who have faith in the people's power and are capable of harnessing the same. People's power can achieve what the governmental power may not.

But even governmental power can be made to feel the pressure of people's power. At least once the same was done during 1974-75. Though not so visible, people's power is asserting itself again and again through what is now famously known as the anti-incumbency factor. Therefore, no despondency is warranted.

And it is not warranted at all if one minutely analyses the episode of Smt. Sonia Gandhi withdrawing her claim to the prime ministership of the country. It was people's power at its zenith. Her sycophants, apologists and pseudo-secular supporters may term her act as that of bravery, renunciation and statesmanship but time will prove that it was people's power which compelled her to choose that course. Howsoever happy the bootlickers of Gandhi dynasty may be feeling over the entry of Priyanka and Rahul Gandhi into country's politics, they will soon find the people's power showing the door both to the dynasty and to its followers.

It can be fairly predicted that though not so visible and not so easy to appreciate today, India's democracy will, in the course of the next few years, be showing its buoyancy, thus compelling its rulers to become more accountable to the people. And this will happen mainly in reaction to the old trick of Smt. Indira Gandhi being played on the people by her successors under the leadership of her daughter-in-law. So, ironically Smt. Sonia Gandhi as the successor of the family will be made to repay the debt, which Smt. Indira Gandhi owed to the country.

And the people's power will not stop at that. Hereafter, of whatever hue the governmental dispensation at the centre may be, it will have to take cognisance of the people's aspirations. The country will thus find both the powers – people's as well as governmental taking more care of nation building. The country can rest assured about its bright future.

□

Blessing in Disguise

Like many earlier elections of the states and the centre, the recently concluded one to the 14th Lok Sabha also shattered the calculations of a large number of political analysts, including almost all the pollsters.

The BJP bore the severest brunt. Obviously the BJP camp must be going through the trauma of disbelief and distress. So can it be concluded that the 'feel good' is over for every BJP worker?

Perhaps not. Not perhaps for that selfless worker for whom BJP symbolises an ideology, government or no government. Perhaps for him 'feel good' has come back in the form of a new opportunity, which makes his ideological battle more worthwhile.

Perhaps that committed worker of BJP, who got drawn to it because of its ideology, is feeling good because now he can carry on his ideology without

---

Last part of 3 parts of article, Organiser, 20 June, 2004.

the burden of keeping governmental power intact and making it 'deliver' the goods. Perhaps that tireless worker who is determined to steer ahead without compromising on ideology is really feeling good because the issues which inspire him the most have come to the centre-stage of Indian politics with a bang. All said and done, perhaps in party's defeat, a BJP diehard finds a blessing in disguise because now he can launch on a full-fledged ideological war with full vigour at his command.

A BJP enthusiast may find at least three issues of great relevance to him – the issues of national ethos, national pride and interest and end of dynastic politics.

The first one of the three i.e. the issue of national ethos became the foremost issue for the BJP at least since 1992, the year when the Babri structure was demolished. Since then, an unending debate has been going on in the country on the definition of national ethos. For BJP, the ethos is best represented by the phenomenon called Hindutva. The forces which have joined together to form the government at the centre, taking the advantages of the weaknesses of the democratic process with dubious flaunting of secularism as their main concern, have boastfully claimed that BJP's defeat amounts to rejection of Hindutva. To a BJP worker this provides an excellent opportunity to engage its detractors in a debate to prove to them in particular and the public in general the worth and content of his ideology.

The second issue – that of national pride and interest, is relatively new for a BJP worker. The issue has emerged on the national scene as that of national shame being felt and national interest being mortgaged as a consequence of the occupation of Prime Minister's post by a person of foreign origin, i.e. Smt. Sonia Gandhi. Till the election results were out, the issue was in the realm of theoretical possibility but soon after, it almost became a hard reality but for the instant outcry and protests made throughout the country. Though the country has got temporary relief, the possibility still lurks. The BJP worker may find it worthwhile to initiate a fight to finish the battle on the issue.

The third issue – that of ending of dynastic politics, is both new and old for a BJP worker. The issue particularly relates to stalling the Nehru-Gandhi dynasty from demeaning India's democracy and heralding of healthy and principled politics. The issue may be as important to a BJP worker as the first two.

□

The Unsung Heroes of the Emergency

It began sometime during November-December 1973 in Gujarat. Due to inflation, an engineering college raised the mess bill for hostellers. There were strong protests. Other colleges in the state also raised the mess bills on the same account. Protests became widespread and grew strong to turn into a movement. Corruption was held responsible for inflation. It became a movement against inflation and corruption. The pinch of inflation and corruption was not confined to students alone; the movement became a public movement.

Who was to be held responsible for the problems? Obviously, the government. The movement turned against the state government and the Chief Minister. It was termed as Navnirman Andolan.

Article in *Indian Express* on 26 June, 2020 on the anniversary of Emergency of 1975.

The Unsung Heroes of the Emergency

The pinch of inflation and corruption was not confined to Gujarat. By February 1974, students in Bihar rose into action. There, too, the state government and Chief Minister were held responsible. In March, the movement started in Bihar. In order to curb it, the government used force. This added fuel to the fire. Both in Gujarat and Bihar, it was students leading the movement. Inflation and corruption were not confined to the two states. The movement started spreading to other parts of the country, though Bihar became the epicentre. Jayaprakash Narayan (JP), a Gandhian and a Sarvodaya leader, lived in Bihar. He had grown old and had decided to spend the rest of his life involved in constructive activities in a limited area in Bihar. The student leaders of Bihar knew the worth of both – the issues being raised and JP. They knew that if JP came forward to bless them, the movement would gain respectability. And JP did bless them.

Once JP did that, the state government went berserk. JP was *lathi*-charged when he led a demonstration in Patna but JP was a mature and seasoned statesman. He ensured non-violent methods of protest and took the movement out of Bihar to make it a national movement. It did not remain confined to students. Four non-Congress non-communist political parties (Bharatiya Jan Sangh, Congress (O), Socialist Party and Bharatiya Lok Dal) became active in the movement. And the JP movement was born.

As the movement started picking up, the Central Government and the then Prime Minister Indira Gandhi were held responsible for the corruption and inflation. But JP did not confine himself to these two issues. He pointed at the other malaises in public life and gave a call for 'total revolution'. He called upon the central government to address the issues.

From March 1974 to June 1975, the movement went through different phases and a lot of political activities took place. All said and done, it was a national movement against the central government in general, and the PM in particular. In her own way, Indira Gandhi tried to diffuse the situation, but she failed. She had been in power for nearly four years and the movement leaders asked for her resignation.

The flashpoint came on 12 June, 1975, when two major developments took place. Earlier in March, the movement had achieved a partial victory when the Chief Minister of Gujarat resigned, paving way for fresh assembly elections. On June 12, his party lost in the election which provided a fillip for the national movement. Simultaneously, on June 12, Indira Gandhi lost an election petition against her wherein she had been charged for malpractices in her election to Lok Sabha in 1971. For the movement, the demand for her resignation became logical. As she had lost in the High Court, she preferred to go to Supreme Court and stuck to her post. Though a minor one, Indira Gandhi got yet another jolt on June 12 – the death of her important political aide, D.P. Dhar.

The battle entered its crucial phase. Forces on both sides strengthened themselves. Indira Gandhi decided to continue as PM as the Supreme Court had granted her partial stay so far as her Lok Sabha seat was concerned. It facilitated her continuation as PM. JP, on the other hand, called for a rally at Ramlila Maidan in Delhi on June 25 to announce his future course of action.

It was a massive rally. A call was given for a satyagraha to commence from June 29. JP asked the police and defence forces not to obey illegal orders from Indira Gandhi. Though it was a simple statement, it was used against him for allegging that he was calling upon the police and defence forces to revolt against the government.

On the same day, at midnight, internal Emergency was declared. In fact, the ruling party had been considering the idea since the beginning of the year. Two things were done immediately – several eminent leaders were arrested and censorship was imposed on the media on that night itself. In the days after, the media was not free to report. Anything that was to be published had to be cleared by the censor authorities. What it implied was that nothing against the government would go in print. Those who dared to disobey were punished in one form or another.

The number of persons who were arrested

kept swelling day by day. People who belonged to parties and organisations which were supporting the movement were arrested. Three types of arrests were made. The most stringent were made under the Maintenance of Internal Security Act (MISA), which allowed the government to detain anyone whom it considered necessary. As the title of the law suggests, the arrest was made for the maintenance of internal security. It was preventive detention. The duration of arrest was also in the hands of the government. The second type of arrests were made under the Defence of India Rules (DIR). Such an arrest could be made when someone was found to be involved in activities threatening the law and order of the country. An arrest was to be made for a real act endangering law and order, and the arrested person had to be prosecuted for the offence in a court of law. A large-scale mockery of the law was made at the instance of Congress leaders. People were identified for arrest, false charges were levelled against them and they were put behind the bars.

Then there was the third category of arrests–the mildest one. Some minor charges would be levelled and persons would be arrested. This scene lingered on for months. Those opposed to the Emergency developed their own ways of opposing it. Underground activities and literature, and over-ground *satyagraha* in opposition to the Emergency were the two tools adopted.

The Unsung Heroes of the Emergency

As JP had been arrested on the first night itself, the leadership of the movement came in the hands of Nanaji Deshmukh, the veteran leader of the Bharatiya Jana Sangh (the earlier incarnation of BJP). In late August 1975, Nanaji, who had been successful in avoiding arrest till then, was nabbed. Thereafter, the leadership fell in the hands of Dattopant Thengdi – a veteran trade union leader. Beginning in October 1975, a nationwide *satyagraha* was launched. Around 1,00,000 people courted arrest.

The Emergency and the battle against it went on till the end of 1976. Various efforts were also made to diffuse the situation but to no result. As a person, Indira Gandhi was a strong-headed ruler. Democracy was nowhere to be experienced in the country. The Lok Sabha's period had been extended earlier by one year to delay the election which became due in early 1976. Then came January 1977. The Emergency was relaxed and Lok Sabha elections were held in March 1977. Much to her astonishment, not only her party was defeated, but Indira Gandhi and her son Sanjay Gandhi could not get elected to Lok Sabha.

It's important to know why Indira Gandhi opted to impose the Emergency. She had already ruled the country for over four years and to fulfil the demand of democracy, she could have ordered fresh Lok Sabha elections. But she was not a 'democrat'. She was an autocrat whom political developments had catapulted to the top post in the country. Her authoritarian traits started unfolding when she split her party in 1969 and captured the top position in the party and the government. To her advantage, the opposition parties had miserably failed in challenging her in the 1971 Lok Sabha election, which she won with a thumping majority. Another development at the end of 1971 – the war with Pakistan and the creation of Bangladesh – further increased her popularity. She would accept no challenge to her supremacy. She preferred confrontationist politics.

A legitimate question can be asked: Why did she choose to go in for elections in 1977? There were several reasons. Though she was an autocrat, she was not an absolute dictator. Nor was the governmental machinery suitable for dictatorship. She had grown up in a democratic country, which had seen five Lok Sabha elections, the last one going in her favour in a big way, and the sixth had become overdue. It is also said that she was fairly confident of winning the election.

It is also pertinent to note that a certain socio-political force played a key role in the developments before and during the Emergency. It was the Sangh Parivar, which has been denied its due in the historical evaluation of events.

The Gujarat movement in beginning was a spontaneous one, but it survived because of the major role played by the ABVP [Akhil Bharatiya Vidyarthi Parishad]. The Bihar movement was a creation of ABVP. It were leaders of the ABVP and the RSS – Ram

Bahadur Rai and K.N. Govindacharya – who roped in JP. In the JP movement, the ABVP, Bharatiya Jana Sangh (which was biggest amongst the four parties supporting the movement) and the rest of the Sangh Parivar played a leading role. During the Emergency, it was Deshmukh and Thengdi (founder of the Bharatiya Mazdoor Sangh, a trade union affiliate of the Sangh Parivar) who led the underground movement. In the *satyagraha*, the largest contributor was the RSS and the Parivar.

□

Youth as the Bulwark

Akhil Bharatiya Vidyarthi Parishad (ABVP) is the premier and the foremost student organisation in the country with many unique features. While it is the only genuine student organisation which is not a wing of any political party, it is also a regular and full-fledged forum of floating membership with active involvement of teachers as its long-term functionaries. ABVP has the distinction of discovering the role that students can play in a society and has the credit of playing such a role as well. It is the ABVP today, which, because of its credible past, enjoys the confidence of a large number of well-meaning citizens with regard to the country's future. To understand the success story of ABVP, a brief peep into its history is worthwhile.

The birth of ABVP was a case of premature delivery. Founded in 1948, to meet the exigency of the then situation arising out of the unexpected incident

---

Published in Organiser weekly on 15 August, 2004.

of Mahatma Gandhi's murder and consequent ban on RSS, the ABVP had the distinction of being the first organisation of RSS school of thought to be created. But the exigency was the immediate, not the basic, reason. It was a visionary step taken before time under compelling circumstances. After India became independent, the RSS leaders started thinking of best ways of contributing in the task of national reconstruction. The idea of encouraging swayamsevaks to enter different fields of social life to serve the cause through them took shape in Sangh leaders' minds. But before any concrete steps could be taken, the organisation was banned. So immediately a way had to be found to minimise the impact of the ban and continue with the mission. Students and youth were the backbone of the organisation. So it was decided to float a students' organisation in the country under whose auspices the mission would go on. Nearly four months after the ban, ABVP came into existence in early June 1948. For about a year, till the ban was lifted in early July 1949, RSS work was indirectly carried on under its auspices.

Once the ban was over, the original idea of swayamsevaks working in different walks of life became implementable. So ABVP started working, keeping that perspective in mind. Concentrating mainly on bringing college student into its fold, it began serving the country primarily by organising constructive activities. Its organisational network started spreading both at states and national level. The organisation grew slowly and sporadically in the first decade. Not much attention could be paid by RSS to its growth, firstly, due to its main attention on its basic work and on undoing the damage caused by the ban and, secondly, because of more important objectives of sending capable swayamsevaks in the fields of politics and labour unions. The needs of ABVP were addressed in 1958 when Prof. Yashwantrao Kelkar, a teacher in a college in Mumbai, was given its command. Being a very methodical person with a belief in 'slow and steady wins the race', Shri Kelkar firstly concentrated in Mumbai and Maharashtra and then gradually in the rest of the country. It took eight years for the RSS to fulfill the needs of different states. In 1967, the Sangh spared its important workers in different states for the work of ABVP. The intensive and effective journey of ABVP began then.

The period between 1967 and 1975 was the most significant for ABVP for several reasons. Sound organisational methodology in the form of collective team work was adopted along with clear enunciation of three basic principles which ABVP was to scrupulously follow: (i) constructive approach behind all its efforts, (ii) the organisation to remain away from power and party politics; and (iii) students, teachers and educationists taken as one family. Student activism was at its peak in India as well as in other parts of the world. The ABVP actively participated in the same and enriched its knowledge and experience of students' movement. Being a serious forum itself, ABVP made a deep study of potentials of a student organisation and 'discovered' that college-going students can play the role of citizens of today in a society. So ABVP made its original ideological contribution in the field of student activism by declaring that rather than being citizens of tomorrow, the students are very much citizens of today. Very soon ABVP's ideological contribution proved its worth when students played a crucial role in the historic Navanirman movement of Gujarat and JP movement of Bihar in the years of 1974-75. Not merely that, it was ABVP itself which became the backbone of former movement and initiator and key player of the latter. It was ABVP, which impressed upon Shri Jayaprakash Narayan to lend his support to the Bihar movement. Once convinced Shri Narayan not only supported the movement, he gradually became its leader. The movement did not remain confined to Bihar. It spread to different parts of the country. The then Prime Minister Smt. Indira Gandhi, who was the main target of the movement, became so furious that she imposed internal Emergency in the country which took nearly 21 months to come to an end. The ABVP was all along an important participant in the movement and in the struggle against Emergency. It also actively participated in the elections to Lok Sabha in early 1977 for the defeat of Congress and victory of Janata Party because the election was the real battle between dictatorship and democracy.

The rest of the story of ABVP's history is the story of impressive growth of a clear-headed organisation. Armed with its three basic principles and equally important organisational methodology and faith in the philosophy of students being citizens of today, the ABVP marched on and on after 1977. It played important roles on various national issues and contributed in the nation-building task in its own way. It became a thriving and purposeful national students' organisation with its branches in every nook and corner of the country. Active on all the 365 days of an year, it became a living instrument for thousands of students to serve the country through an impressive list of constructive, agitational and representative activities and a host of important projects. ABVP's march is still on.

□

Catch them Young for Democracy

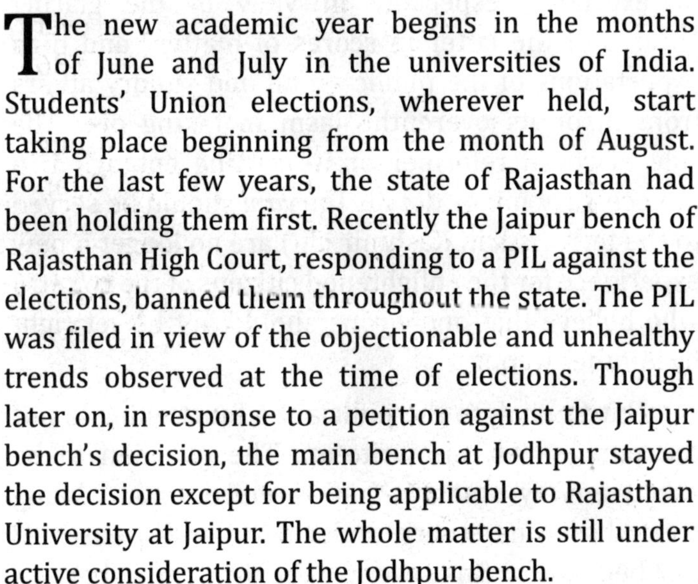

The new academic year begins in the months of June and July in the universities of India. Students' Union elections, wherever held, start taking place beginning from the month of August. For the last few years, the state of Rajasthan had been holding them first. Recently the Jaipur bench of Rajasthan High Court, responding to a PIL against the elections, banned them throughout the state. The PIL was filed in view of the objectionable and unhealthy trends observed at the time of elections. Though later on, in response to a petition against the Jaipur bench's decision, the main bench at Jodhpur stayed the decision except for being applicable to Rajasthan University at Jaipur. The whole matter is still under active consideration of the Jodhpur bench.

Nevertheless, one cannot resist the comment

Written for Organiser weekly on 31 July, 2005 for Youth Folio Section.

that the decision of Jaipur bench was yet another classic example of a patient being killed in order to kill the disease. It was not for the first time, neither in Rajasthan, nor thinking of other parts of the country, that students' union elections were considered unnecessary, undesirable and dispensable. In fact in large parts of the country, such elections are either not held or have met the same fate as was desired by the Jaipur bench. So why find fault with the bench's judgment?

Judiciary taking over the task of legislature or executive, especially in view of the glaring failures of the latter in scores of matters and high expectations of the public on all and sundry affairs from it, or its overenthusiasm in taking over the role of social reformer or its getting entangled in unnecessary minor details (*biryani* should be served to the terrorists in Kashmir jail) are no longer a new experience for the enlightened citizens of the country who believe that one wrong should not be set right by another wrong.

But to analyse the judiciary's functioning is not the purpose of this write-up. The question to be asked is why students' union elections are being treated as unnecessary, undesirable or dispensable? Just because we find several unhealthy and abhorring features associated with elections and functioning of the unions, so do they become inessential? Just because many union leaders do not measure up to the expectations, so should the unions be declared undesirable? Just because governmental or educational authorities can write off the unions with one stroke of pen, so do they become dispensable? A thorough probing is warranted.

Politics and Logic of Students' Union Election

Do we not see the same malaise, as seen in the case of students' unions, associated even to a greater extent, with elections and functioning of parliament, state legislatures or local bodies? As we look around, elections take place for a large mass of social bodies, such as: (i) political parties (ii) professional or occupational organisations, e.g. employees' unions, traders' associations, etc., (iii) religious organisations, e.g. SGPC, ramlila committees, etc. (iv) sports and cultural organisations, or clubs, etc., such as BCCI, (v) service organisations which run schools, colleges, hospitals and *dharamshalas*, etc., (vi) economic interest organisations, e.g. joint stock companies or cooperatives etc., and (vii) communities or caste organisations, etc. Do we find their elections and functioning being very healthy with no ills afflicting them? If not, should not such elections be dispensed with?

When we closely observe the elections of bodies of even elite occupational groups, such as industrialists, lawyers, doctors, teachers or chartered accountants etc. or of elite academic and professional institutions, such as university senates or syndicates, Bar Council of India or Medical Council of India, etc., we often come across one or other abhorring features associated with their elections also. So should not their elections also be dispensed with?

The desirability and importance of students' unions can be appreciated only if the relevance and necessity of democracy is accepted. Though legitimate doubts can be raised about the efficacy of democracy, yet it can be firmly said that only shortsighted, impatient or cynical persons consider democracy or elections as a luxury. Despite all its weaknesses, democracy is considered as the best, or least harmful system that the human society has evolved for itself, especially when long-run healthy and orderly growth of a society has to be taken care of. Though a long essay may be warranted to justify one's point yet avoiding that, this write-up is being proceeded with presuming that democracy's desirability is unquestionable.

Once the need of democracy is understood, then can we think of democracy without elections? If elections are necessary, is it desirable to have them in selected cases? If national and larger social existence is comprised by variety of lower-level entities, then can the latter function smoothly without elected bodies?

Democracy cannot take roots if it is practiced selectively. More than being a formal system and mere tool of governmental formation, democracy has to be looked at as a value of life. Democracy means a certain behavioural attitude, mindset and temperament. The more it is practiced and experienced the more its worth is understood and learnt. Practicing it once in a while or in a half-hearted way only weakens democracy rather than strengthening it.

Clarity about democracy leads us towards the desirability of students' unions. Students' unions have had a long history. Perhaps unions at college or university level used to be there even before independence. Unions along with their elections provide first-ever lesson of democratic functioning to the students. Unions, while providing opportunities to students to manage many of their own affairs themselves, have served in the past and can serve many useful purposes with regard to promotion of leadership quality, protection of legitimate interests of students, redressal of their grievances, achievement of needed amenities and conducting whole lot of programmes and activities which are of interests or are useful to them and which unfold their potentials, talents and creativities, etc.

Over and above such things, unions can prove useful platforms for playing of students' role in national and larger social issues. Wherever, and to the extent, possible, the unions can take up service projects or schemes for the benefit of society in general also.

We should not forget that most of the college-going students in India today are of the 18+ age which means they are already eligible voters for the purpose of parliamentary and assembly elections, etc. If democracy is learned through practice, then should not such voters get the opportunity of experiencing it in their own institutions?

But what about the unhealthy trends and practices that we find associated with the unions, the question may be asked.

The answer is not difficult. Controlling of malaise that afflicts students' unions and their elections is not as difficult as it is made out to be. Ways and means can be found for the same by authorities, provided they have vision and will power. But first a note of caution. Too many laws and restrictions can prove unimplementable and counterproductive. Healthy practices in a society can never be enforced merely by making laws or by high handedness. They are best achieved by raising the average level of social consciousness of its members.

Democracy in its present form is new to India, only 53-years old. We should not forget that England, which is presented as the best model of democracy, had to spend centuries for maturing of its democracy, that too, when it had a far smaller size of population than India has and had all the resources of world at its command for a very long time. Even today, British democracy is found to be wanting in certain respects, at least on the front of availability of equal status and opportunities to its womenfolk.

Coming back to controlling of malaise, the first and foremost thing that needs to be done is to make the students aware of the importance of democracy. Societies survive on the strength of idealism and values and if democracy is a value of life, then who is most suited to uphold and protect that value? None other than students and youth. Youth are always considered as best practitioners of idealism and values and students make the easily identifiable core of youth. So the country will only gain by arousing their idealism. If the students' unions have become the tools of unscrupulous elements, they also provide opportunities to idealists to catch the bull by its horns. Evil is always defeated by good.

Some of the ways and means that can keep the malaise within reasonable limits can be: restrictions related to personal eligibility for contestants may be imposed, such as maximum age, minimum marks obtained in the examination last passed, no failing in any examination, no conviction for any offence, etc. and related to electioneering, such as no use of posters, banners, hoardings, no offering of gifts to the voters, no use of loudspeakers, restricted use of vehicles, etc. Being postgraduate students or having been elected leaders at college level in the past may be made eligibilities for contesting university union elections. One can think of more such things.

The experience suggests that a direct election proves better than indirect election in checkmating the corrupt electoral practices. Also, it has been amply proved that unions with nominated meritorious students hardly function. Elections alone bring forth the type of activism required in a leader.

In addition, serious student organisations and responsible political leaders can be urged and taken into confidence for making elections as free from vices as feasible.

□

Clean Politics Key to ABVP Success

The victory of Akhil Bharatiya Vidyarthi Parishad (ABVP) candidates for all the four posts of Delhi University Students' Union, election for which was held on September 12 is significant in more than one respect. ABVP won all the posts after 13 years though it had won them several times before.

The organisation started participating in the election regularly since 1968. In 1971, it won the President's post and thereafter its victory spree started. Most of the years, it captured most of the posts.

For three consecutive years 1973, 1974 and 1977, it got all the posts. (Election was not held in 1975 and 1976 due to internal emergency). It withdrew from the election between 1978 and 1981. But during that period a student front named Janata Vidyarthi

---

Hindustan Times, 8 October, 1997.

Morcha (JVM) came into existence which had the support of ABVP. JVM took part in the election and its victories were equally impressive.

In 1982, the ABVP joined the fray again in alliance with JVM and won all the posts for three consecutive years till 1984. 1985 was its worst year when it got only Secretary's post but within two years it regained the lost ground and from 1987 onwards in most of the years it got three out of four posts. JVM withdrew from the fray after 1987.

Before going into the significance of this year's result, it would be appropriate to go into the reasons of unchallenged supremacy of ABVP for all these years. The most important reason has been the non-corruptability of the voters. System of direct election was introduced from 1973. Since a very large number of voters, between 30 to 40 thousand elect the office bearers directly, it becomes impossible for any candidate or organisation to rig or unduly influence the election. In such a dispensation, the ABVP always proves superior to its traditional competitor NSUI. In view of its better image and organisational network, it outsmarts NSUI.

But a queer and unhealthy phenomenon started dominating the election over the last several years. The partial significance of ABVP's victory this year lies in beating that phenomenon.

Due to participation of girl candidates in the

election, it was experienced that their victory was almost sure, whichever side they contested from. NSUI started relying on this advantage while ABVP found it hard to beat. Actually it was ABVP which started fielding at least one girl candidate in its panel ever since 1974 with a positive approach of involving the girls in to the office-bearers team of DUSU. Very soon the queer phenomenon became visible. In order to avoid its humiliation and take the advantage of the said phenomenon, the NSUI started putting up more girls in its panel irrespective of their other merits (for the last six years it fielded only the girls for president's post and generally had two girls in its panel). Though ABVP has always been in favour of encouraging girls' participation in student unions and it always fielded at least one girl candidate, it was never inclined to encash upon the unhealthy phenomenon. This year it gave a crushing blow to that factor and the two girls of NSUI were defeated by the boys.

ABVP's victory this year has another significance also. Perhaps very few people know that the organisation had been insisting for reforms in DUSU election for the last few years. It was because of ABVP's sole efforts that a code of conduct was issued by the university authorities last year. The major requirement under the code was to shun the posters. The ABVP adhered to this norm last year as well as this year while NSUI broke it on last but one day last year and from the very beginning this year. Yet the

ABVP succeeded in the election.

The above mentioned voluntary efforts of ABVP to raise the electoral battle to a higher plain still do not reveal the significance of this year's election result in full measure. It would be a folly to treat this year's result as a chance affair. As a matter of fact, the ABVP has been working in the students' field with a sense of purpose and missionary zeal. It takes the whole issue of students' union and their activities very seriously.

It trains and motivates its cadre to view the whole exercise in that perspective. It so happened that over the years, several ills, many of them being not in control of ABVP, became dominant in DUSU functioning, activities and elections. In the last few years, the ABVP took serious note of them and started gearing up itself to fight against them. A code of conduct was adopted within the organisation also. Its cadre was mentally prepared to tread the difficult but sensible path. The lofty approach and perseverance of the recent years galvanised its cadre in such a way that this year they worked with more precision, zeal and high motivation. And that made the difference. Lest it should miss the attention of not so keen observers of DUSU elections, the whole election campaign of ABVP was managed by its local unit. Even its national leaders had limited involvement in the organisation of the affair.

The political party, supposed to be close to ABVP,

was neither at its beck and call nor was it needed in the matter. On the other hand, the whole leadership of Congress and NSUI took active interest in the electioneering and party leaders took meetings and issued statements and appeals in favour of NSUI candidates. Even Mrs Sonia Gandhi was dragged into the affair. A colourful poster showing Sonia and NSUI president Alka Lamba together urged upon the voters to vote for NSUI.

□

DUSU Election 2003
What went wrong with ABVP?

The National Students Union of India (NSUI) won a landslide victory in the recent Delhi University Students' Union elections while the Akhil Bharatiya Vidyarthi Parishad (ABVP) faced its worst defeat ever. The outcome of the poll was not unexpected for the observers. They knew it well that certain well-defined factors have become crucial determinants in such elections. If you do follow certain norms, you will win; and if you miss out on them, then you will lose.

The DUSU electoral battles have always been a contest between the NSUI and the ABVP. The ABVP has usually emerged the stronger because of its better performance, image and organisational abilities. Factors that help the contestants are: one, proper publicity of their names, so that they are

---

Published in *Pioneer Daily* on 26 September, 2003.

'known' to the voters, and, two, a female candidate always stands a better chance of winning than a male. Another factor is the party's arrangement on the polling day. Slips with names of the contestants, if distributed before a voter enters the booth, have a positive effect, as they are handy for reference to names and ballot numbers.

Two elements influence the outcome:

1. Nearly 40 per cent of voters are new entrants in the university. Such students for the first time are face-to face with students' organisations and elections in less than two months of their entry into colleges. They are excited to vote and get carried away by these factors.

2. The said factors carry more weight for senior students also than other issues like ideology, manifestos and activities of the students' organisations or the performance of the outgoing office-bearers.

This year, the NSUI had a clear advantage as far as the first factor was concerned. The names of its candidates for the top three posts were known well in advance. Except that, whether one agrees or not, this year's electoral outcome, especially the NSUI's victory margins, can be summed up as: one, the Congress and the Delhi government ruled by it won, while the genuine students' organisation of the country lost; two, the approach of 'win-at-any-cost' was victorious, while 'fight-but-adhere-to-norms' was the loser's approach.

NSUI aspirants were already known because one of them was joint secretary of DUSU a year ago, the second was a member of the outgoing DUSU executive, and the third had contested for DUSU presidentship last year. Their names were highlighted throughout the year or immediately after the new academic year commenced through individual posters. While campaigning, they launched an un-precedented poster and pamphlet war. Also, party functionaries turned up in large numbers outside the polling booths for distribution of slips.

The ABVP, being an idealistic organisation, while taking cognisance of the dominant factors, tried to keep off from their degrading features. It could not, and beyond an extent did not want to, compete with the rivals on these counts. Its aspirants are not allowed to issue their posters till they become candidates, so their names were not known beforehand. The known names of the ABVP, those of the outgoing DUSU secretary and vice president, who would have been formidable challengers to the NSUI, could not become candidates this year. So far as the poster and pamphlets were concerned, the ABVP remained within its resources and self-imposed limits. Last, the ABVP could not match the Congress cadres outside the polling booths because it did not want to politicise the affair to the extent the NSUI did.

DUSU Election 2003 What went wrong with ABVP?

In popular perception, the ABVP is considered to be a wing of the BJP. However, the truth is different. It is a unique students' organisation, which has, from the very beginning, chosen the path of becoming a full-fledged students' organisation with emphasis on patriotism, nationalism, idealism and values of life. Not becoming a wing of a political party is one of its basic principles. It maintains its independence from the BJP and refrains from seeking involvement of the party. Though it has an ideological closeness to the BJP, since both belong to the same school of thought, and takes its support when necessary, it makes a clear demarcation between itself and the party.

The ABVP has been in the DUSU electoral fray since 1968 and has won most of the elections due to its genuine and consistent work. It will retrieve its lost ground in no time.

□

NSUI won DUSU Election 2007 by Manipulation

Prof. Raj Kumar Bhatia has been national president of Akhil Bharatiya Vidyarthi Parishad (ABVP). He is now Associate Professor of Economics at DAV College in Delhi. He has been active in Delhi University since 1967 and has closely monitored the Delhi University Students' Union (DUSU) elections for the last more than three decades. A representative from *Organiser* weekly, spoke to him in New Delhi to find out the reasons behind the defeat of ABVP in the recent DUSU elections. Below are the given excerpts:

Why did the ABVP lose all four seats to NSUI in DUSU elections?

It all happened because of the one provision of Lyngdoh Committee that was abruptly implemented in Delhi University (DU) and that too very late after

---

Interview to Organiser weekly, 30 September, 2007.

the election process had started. The election process began on August 2. A meeting of the university officials was held when a decision to implement only one provision was made. The colleges and students came to know about this decision only on August 23 whereas August 24th was the last date for filing the nominations. I feel it was a deliberate plan on part of the DU officials, particularly the Election Officer, in collusion with Congress leaders. They messed up the whole thing. They implemented only one provision of Lyngdoh Committee, which says that there should be no academic arrears of the candidate.

The whole game plan was that the university authorities were bent upon providing help to the Congress and its students' wing, NSUI. For the last few years, some top Congress leaders like Oscar Fernandes and others were taking more interest in this election and many months in advance they had formulated detailed plans to win the elections. The Congress candidate for presidential post had no academic arrear. She is the daughter of a professor of law. Her mother is a High Court advocate and the Chief Election Officer happens to be a friend of her parents. Therefore, they all, in order to hijack the elections, made this plan. This provision of no academic arrears was used against the proposed ABVP candidate, whose name was almost known to everyone. This provision, which needed to be interpreted specifically in the context of Delhi

University, proved helpful for the NSUI candidate as the interpretation was tailor-made to debar ABVP candidate from contesting.

But you should have gone to the court.

Yes, we immediately went to Delhi High Court. The University tried to mislead the Court to hide its guilt. But the Court did not go into the mischievous game plan of the University and merely confined itself to fractured implementation of the Lyngdoh Committee. There is one major recommendation of the Lyngdoh Committee that the University Union should represent all students, including Ph.D. students. But, fact is that many of the colleges (about 20) including most of the girls' colleges and prestigious St. Stephen's College and Daulat Ram College are not affiliated to the DUSU. The University did not implement this condition of Lyngdoh Committee. Selective implementation of the Lyngdoh Committee created a mess. The University officials simply wanted to hold the election. Therefore, many of the college elections could not be held and the elections are being held again now because the Lyngdoh Committee says if some seats fall vacant within a short time of the election, the by-elections should be held. By-elections are being held in many colleges now. It is because of the mess that was created. In the wake of the mischievous implementations of the Lyngdoh Committee, the whole election was hijacked, which I call the rape of democracy.

The recommendations of Lyngdoh Committee came about one year back. If ABVP respects those recommendations, why did it not field the candidates as per the Lyngdoh Committee's recommendations?

That was not necessary because if those conditions were to be implemented, the University should have informed accordingly in advance. Notification was issued on August 2 and there was nothing like this in that notification. From the next day they invited nominations based on the old nomination form of DUSU elections, which were filled as per a particular proforma issued by the University. In that proforma the students had to give some undertakings. The students should have been told to clear their pending academic arrears in that proforma. The conditions, on which you are going to conduct elections, must have been made clear at the time of notification. The match had already been started and in the middle, the rules of the game were changed. Many times, the University authorities were asked by the media, students, etc., whether they are going to implement the Lyngdoh Committee recommendations. Once a University official clearly said that the elections would not be held on the basis of the Lyngdoh Committee.

The Lyngdoh Committee's recommendations were implemented this year. But the ABVP has

not been performing well in DUSU elections for the last four years. Why?

For that we made a lot of planning this year. To make up our shortfall, this time we were fully prepared. But those preparations were not helpful to us in view of abrupt, illegal and politically motivated implementation of just one condition of Lyngdoh Committee. But despite that, we have improved the vote percentage this year, but this is not the central point. The central point is how the elections are conducted and that was totally unfair. Shri Lyngdoh has also criticised this kind of implementation of his recommendations in DU.

□

Non-student Youth Organisation: Dire Need of the Country

A society's, country's or nation's progress depends on the efforts of government as well as of the non-governmental organisations. It is a general belief that non-governmental organisations play a very important role in a situation when government fails in performing its duties.

It is also an undisputed fact that between different sections of society the youth has the greater capability of serving a society, especially keeping in view the future of a society. The future quality of life in a society depends more on what youth thinks and what kind of society it strives for. Collective thinking and collective efforts of the youth can and do lay down the foundation stone on

Published in Organiser weekly on 30 January, 2011.

which a future society rests.

When we think of a society, we find that apart from the government, several social organisations function in that society and a society is always benefitted from purposeful social organisations. Also it is found that depending on society's current requirements, new organisations are needed.

Keeping the above analysis in mind, there has been a strong feeling that there is a dire need in our country for a non-governmental, non-party and non-student youth organisation. One finds that such an organisation, if it comes up, can bring about qualitative change in the life of the country.

Two questions need to be answered: first (i) who comprises of non-student youth, and (ii) are there no such organisations already in the country?

Let's take the first question. Generally people below the age of 35 and above 15 are considered youth. But the upper age in Indian context can be stretched to 40 in view of the absence of strong and genuine youth organisations while lower age should start from 20, in order to concentrate on non-students.

Now the second question related to the existing organisations. This writer is aware of three organisations in the field: Vishwa Yuvak Kendra, Nehru Yuva Kendra Sanghathan and National Yuva

Cooperative Society; though few more may be there. But in the knowledge of the writer none of them measures to the expectations being expressed here. Of the known organisations, the first one is an elite organisation with limited reach, second one is a governmental organisation having all the limitations and weaknesses of the government sponsored institutions and the third is engaged in pursuing limited agenda of creating self-employment opportunities for the youth.

Assuming that such an organisation is created, what exactly is expected of it? Firstly, the organisation should be created at the all India level on the principle of cadre-based mass organisation, i.e. it should have a core cadre committed to its objectives but it should have a mass following amongst the youth. Such an effective organisation can be created only when rural youth and ordinary urban youth are roped into it. Secondly, the organisation should keep itself scrupulously away from supporting a political party. Needless to say that political parties already have their youth fronts which are capable of taking care of their respective parties. Thirdly, the whole effort should be made with a constructive approach with the positive target of nation building.

What are the nation building activities? Broadly two types of activities should be taken up – constructive and the activities aimed at raising public awareness or agitational ones for desired objectives.

In public life, constructive activities always deserve utmost importance. Apart from being desirable in themselves, they help in grooming responsible holistic members of a society. Cynics, critics or indifferent people do not serve a society as much as the constructive activists do.

Scores of constructive activities can be thought of which a youth organisation may take up. To cite a few of them: i) service activities for the needy sections, like free medical aid, library and reading rooms, literacy, micro financing, skills needed for gainful employment, blood donations, shelters for homeless etc.; ii) book banks, coaching classes, scholarships, career counselling etc. for students; iii) promotion of talents of youth through personality development camps or in sports, arts, general knowledge, etc.; iv) strengthening of national integration through inter-state visits, etc.

Youth's role and potential have always been recognised with respect to its being upholder of ideals and values, watchdog of society's interests and deterrent and crusader against ills. It is in this context that the youth organisation should take up activities aimed at raising public awareness and creating pressures to elicit desired results. Such activities may be 'for' desirable things, like environment protection, sustainable consumption, spirituality, *swadeshi*, national security, democracy, human rights, gender equality, accountability and transparency; or 'against' undesirable things like terrorism and violence, infiltration, corruption, poverty, unemployment, economic disparities, parochialism of different types, social evils like untouchability, casteism, dowry, and female foeticide, etc.

One problem is faced by the youth under reference. After finishing studies, youth enter two phases of life almost simultaneously – occupational life and married life. Both these phases require lot of time and attention from youth for proper settlement. Often those youth who might have been active in social life during their student days withdraw from public activism precisely on account of such pressures. But can such a withdrawal be justified? Onc can understand the pressures but social obligations warrant that a youth should consciously find time for social work. For such youth, sparing time should become less important than remaining committed to fulfilling the duty towards the society. Where there is a will there is a way. For them it should become a matter of balancing three obligations – social, occupational and domestic and socially conscious youth are always able to do it.

Now who will bell the cat? This writer has only

underlined a social need. Only time will tell whether someone fulfils it or not. One thing is sure: whoever takes up this challenging task, he or she will have to work hard and will require a time span of five to 10 years to realise the dream.

□

Let Truth Prevail in Gujarat

It was the heart leading the head. It often happens with a human being. It happens more if the human being is a poet. And the chances of its happening increase further when the poet is sitting in the lap of nature. The surroundings provide wings to his heart. This is what happened in the case of the poet, former Prime Minister of India in Manali, when his 'secular' heart left behind his 'Hindu' head.

There the two-year old lie that Narendra Modi was responsible for anti-Muslim riots after the Godhra incident and a few days old canard that BJP/NDA lost Lok Sabha elections because of the riots succeeded in touching the chords of the poet's heart and in overtaking the hard facts, which his head had known pretty well, that the riots were the

---

Written in Organiser weekly on 27 June, 2004, this piece refers to heart of Shri AB Vajpayee and head of Shri KS Sudarshan. Vajpayee had held Narendra Modi, the then CM of Gujarat responsible for BJP's debacle in 2004 Lok Sabha election whom Sudershan had defended.

consequence of ghastly burning of innocent Ram *bhaktas* in Godhra and Narendra Modi had done his best to control them and the riots were no reason for the Lok Sabha debacle.

The lie almost ousted the truth. The senior darling of Hindus was prepared to sacrifice the junior one because his heart wished so.

But the course was corrected quickly. Head came forward to lead the heart. It also happens with a human being. It happens more if the human being is a philosopher. And the chances of its happening increase further when the philosopher is sitting on the land of *karmayogis*. The surroundings provided wings to his head. This is what happened in the case of philosopher Sarsanghchalak of RSS in Nagpur, when his 'secular' head remained in control of his 'Hindu' heart. There the hard facts succeeded in touching the brainwaves of the philosopher's head and in pushing back the lie that his heart had felt pretty well.

The truth prevailed over the lie. Another senior darling of the Hindus saved the junior one from being made the sacrificial goat because his head told that was the right course.

□

A Soliloquy: Good Soul Self-defeated

There was a pious soul, who knew no self-interest and was full of social motivation. It was ever ready to accept any social work that fell on its shoulders. Since the soul was pious, it never bothered to make discrimination between more and less important work or more and less deserving beneficiaries of its benevolence. It was as easily amenable to self-seekers and cunning people as it was to selfless and straightforward persons. It was very generous towards people around it.

Once it so happened that members of its community felt that an organisation needed to be floated to safeguard the community's interests and for its welfare. The pious soul took up the responsibility and established an organisation. Very soon a few more such souls joined it. Together they

Published in Organiser weekly on 19 December, 2004 based on real life experience of an organisation.

ran the organisation and did a lot of social work. Since social work was their main motivation and organisation came afterwards, the former always got precedence over the latter. The organisation did not get as much attention from them as it needed. Also, since discriminating among persons was not in their nature, as it mostly happens, the self-seekers outnumbered the selfless in the organisation. The organisation could not make a healthy start. Nearly a decade rolled by like this.

Apart from its main community, the pious soul was also associated with another community. The latter felt that the soul was quite suitable to become its leader. The soul did not disappoint it. It was not in its nature. Since the soul was comfortably placed because of the other such souls in the first organisation, the organisation's business went on. Poor attention to it by the souls and its exploitation by the self-seekers did not allow the organisation to grow properly. Another decade rolled by in this way.

Yet another community got attracted towards the pious soul and wanted to benefit from its leadership. The soul did not disappoint it too. The only difference it made was that now the soul had no time left for the first organisation, the burden of running which fell squarely on the other good souls. But these souls also were not very different from the first one. So, no qualitative change took place in the functioning of the organisation. More decades rolled by.

A Soliloquy: Good Soul Self-defeated

The organisation ever remained of secondary importance to the leading souls and good pasture for self-seekers. Even after several years of its founding, the organisation remained where it was.

Moral: Being a pious soul does not suffice in a social organisation.

□

Fall in Public Life Values and the Role of Individuals

A few weeks ago Dussehra was celebrated throughout the country. This festival, held every year, highlights the victory of good over evil or of *dharma* over *adharma* and teaches us to be virtuous. Since ages, people have been exhorted to lead a virtuous life and abstain from indulging in vices. One may wonder why this has been done repeatedly. The answer is not difficult. The fight between good and evil or virtue and vice or *dharma* and *adharma* has always been the need of human societies and civilisations because evil has non-ending tendency to assert itself and good has to always come forward to suppress it. There can be no better articulation for such a recurrent need than the one made by no less than Lord Krishna when He said that as and when *dharma* loses its importance and *adharma* starts dominating He takes birth to suppress the latter.

Written in 2007 on demand of a friend in Chennai.

Fall in Public Life Values and the Role of Individuals

The fight between good and evil takes place at various levels and in different forms. One level at which it occurs is that of thoughts, principles, ideals, philosophy and values of life. Such a battle is fought at the ideological and intellectual plain. It takes the shape of making distinction and demarcation between good and evil thoughts, principles and ideals, etc. and of upholding the importance and soundness of the former over latter.

The second level relates to sets of people. Here the fight takes place at the level of action between groups of people who stand in the courts of good and evil. Such courts may be as large as a civilisation, a country, a big organisation or a society or as small as a local-level association, club, organisation or society.

Thirdly, and most importantly, the fight occurs at the level of individuals. Here the individuals carry out the fight within themselves in the form of treading on the difficult path of good and avoiding the slippery one of evil.

A society lives happily as long as good prevails over evil or virtue dominates over vice or *dharma* takes precedence over *adharma*. Such a situation exists when a substantial majority of people follow the path of good, both in thought and action. But such a situation is reached with great difficulty because of several steps that have to be taken prior to it.

For human beings, being good at thoughts level is

easier than putting them into practice. So, first of all, some determined individuals win the fight between good and evil within themselves and become good in practice. They, with strong motivation, commitment and perseverance adhere to high moral values in day-to-day life and avoid falling prey to vices.

Then secondly, a section of these determined individuals do not remain contended by being good themselves; they make efforts to do good things for the society.

Thirdly, some of these do-gooders become so motivated that they strive to swell their ranks and decide to fight against evil.

Last but not the least, a section of these people, which does not get discouraged by the setbacks, gives the final blow to the evil and leads to the victory of the good. It is this latter set of people through whom Lord Krishna takes rebirth.

To sum up, what can be said is that ultimately it is the individuals who form the vanguard of the forces of good, and, whenever evil raises its ugly head and there occurs a fall in public life values, their role becomes crucial.

□

Letters to Editor

1
Indira Gandhi

Sir,

Mrs. Indira Gandhi's personality had such a massive impact on the polity of the country that her death is bound to be viewed and analysed in many ways. Ousting an elected leader in a democratic country by assassinating her, is an anathema to democracy. That she should be killed by a man from the security forces is all the more reprehensible and a matter of serious concern. Mrs. Gandhi's death is an unprecedented loss for her sons, family, friends and the party and any sane person would have his sympathies with them.

But a dispassionate analysis of Mrs. Gandhi's policies and style of functioning compels one to believe that she became a victim of her own machinations. Without having high regard for the wisdom of Sikh and Akali leadership, I feel, Mrs. Gandhi's political manoeuvres in Punjab grievously hurt the feelings of the Sikh community, resulting in her murder by an enraged Sikh. To use a rather paradoxical description, she was ushering in a 'democratic dictatorship' by her family in the country and this was conclusively proved soon after her death, with the appointment of Mr. Rajiv Gandhi as her successor and Prime Minister.

To
Indian Express
1 November, 1984

□

2

Loot and Arson in Delhi on 1st November

Sir,

The outbreak of loot and arson against Sikhs in Delhi on 1 November, 1984, was unprecedented and beyond one's comprehension. It certainly was not only an emotional outburst of the people, who felt immensely aggrieved at the assassination of Mrs. Indira Gandhi. No doubt some Sikhs became jubilant at the death of Mrs. Gandhi and distributed sweets and burnt crackers at which certain Congress (I) workers felt strongly offended but that this should have turned into a large scale orgy of loot and arson merely underlines the utter failure of law and order machinery, strong communal bias which has affected the Congress (I) rank and file in the wake of Punjab situation and general deterioration in communal harmony between Sikhs and Hindus.

Going round the city on that fateful day, one could clearly see policemen allowing full freedom to hooligans and Congress (I) workers inciting them and Hindus in general feeling happy at the development. We can ill afford such communal disharmony. Congress (I) leadership in particular and the Sikh and Hindu leadership owe if to the country for retrieving this situation at the earliest.

To
Hindustan Times
2 November, 1984

□

3
Rajiv Gandhi

Sir,

A news item appeared in your paper, titled 'Doordarshan Lacks Imagination: Rajiv' (HT dated 14 January, 1986). It referred to Rajiv Gandhi's disapproval of his projection on TV. It quoted Rajiv as saying, "I have told them (Doordarshan) very categorically that they should not project me." To me it appears to be a dishonest statement meant for public consumption. In fact the statement falls in line with the cleverly designed publicity campaign unleashed in the country by Rajiv and his aides to build up the former's image. Even if we assume, to give a benefit of doubt to Rajiv, that he is not directly interested in his image building, it is quite obvious that he is not very serious in curbing this practice. Does he want us to believe that he is so helpless in checking the sickening and blatant misuse of the official media which, according to himself, is 'counter-productive'?

He is only worried about 'counter-productive' projection but certainly not about undemocratic, unhealthy, uneven and productive projection.

Yours etc.

To
Hindustan Times
14 January, 1986

□□□